Introduction to Labour Laws in India

By Siva Prasad Bose and Joy Bose

This book is dedicated to all past, present and future employees and workers employed in India.

Contents

Dedication

This book is dedicated to all the past, present and future workers of India.

Preface

Labour laws govern the conditions of work and labour. They are important in preventing exploitation by employers, preventing mass resignations, providing work security, ensuring good working conditions and creating conditions for a happier workforce. There are a number of laws and protection granted in the Indian constitution and in different types of labour laws. As the workplace conditions evolve, so do the labour laws. Hence it is useful to have an overview of the prevailing laws and protections related to labour in India.

In this book, we give an overview of the main labour laws in India, including the newer labour codes introduced in 2019-2020 by the Indian government and their landmark implementation on 21 November 2025. We also focus on practical issues, such as what to do and whom to approach if one is unfairly dismissed from work, as well as newer developments such as the rights of gig and platform workers. This updated edition incorporates the most recent changes in Indian labour law, including the November 2025 implementation of all four Labour Codes and developments in state-level gig worker legislation. It is hoped that this book will help in spreading awareness about the prevailing labour laws among working people.

Acknowledgements

In writing this book, the authors gratefully acknowledge the following sources:

Labour and Industrial Laws Bare Act 2022, Commercial Law Publishers Pvt Ltd, 2022.

The Law Book: Big Ideas Simply Explained. By DK Publishing, 2020

Wikipedia https://www.wikipedia.org/

Ministry of Labour and Employment, Government of India https://labour.gov.in/

Press Information Bureau, Government of India, New Labour Codes 2025, https://www.pib.gov.in/

International Labour Organization, Report on Realizing Decent Work in the Platform Economy, 2024, https://www.ilo.org/

NITI Aayog, India's Booming Gig and Platform Economy, 2022

Chapter 1: Introduction to Labour Laws

In this chapter we introduce the concept of labour laws and overview some of the laws in India and other countries.

1.1 What are Labour Laws

Labour laws govern the conditions for initiation of employment, conditions of work, industrial action or strikes, unions, as well as dismissal from employment.

If an employee is fired unfairly from their job, they can file a complaint with the labour commissioner to get redressal as per the applicable labour laws. Groups of employees forming a union also falls under the labour laws. Industrial disputes between employers and employees, issues related to retrenchment and unfair dismissal, issues related to union formation, etc all fall under the labour laws.

1.2 Evolution of Labour Laws in India

Labour laws in India have evolved from the conditions of British rule and after India's independence through liberalization and after.

Under the British, particularly in the 19th and early 20th century, a number of modern factories were set up in different parts of India, leading to the creation of a labour force and ultimately also a labour movement. A number of labour laws were also set up that often mirrored similar laws in Britain and were generally progressive in nature, seeking to regulate the conditions of work.

Examples of labour related laws laws set up by the British included the Indian Slavery Act 1843, Societies Registration Act 1860, Co-operative Societies Act 1912, the Workmen's Compensation Act 1923, Indian Trade Unions Act, 1926, the Trades Disputes Act 1929, Payment of wages act 1936 and finally the Industrial Employment Standing orders act 1946.

There were also a number of huge labour strikes in India during British rule, indicating the power of the organized sector and the rise of the trade unions. Examples of such strikes include the 1921 Buckingham and Carnatic Mills Strike and the 1928 South Indian Railway Strike.

After India became independent, a number of protections for labour were included in the constitution of India.

Moreover, a number of labour laws were also established soon after independence and the succeeding decades. These included the Industrial Disputes Act 1947, Minimum Wages Act 1948, Factories Act 1948 and State Shops and Establishments Act.

In 2020 the government of India has proposed four codes related to labour laws to simplify the multiple existing labour laws, including the code of wages and industrial relations code.

1.3 International Labour Organization ILO

ILO is one of the constituents of the United Nations or UN, which is the main international body consisting of representatives of all the nations. ILO was founded in 1919 under what was then the League of Nations, precursor to the United Nations. It is responsible for formulating a set of labour standards to which all the countries in the world are aimed to align their labour laws.

It was responsible for the Declaration on Fundamental Principles and Rights at Work, which was adopted in 1998 and included sections on collective bargaining, forced labour, child labour and discrimination. The core conventions include the right to form unions and collective bargaining, industrial action or strikes, abolition of forced labour and child labour, and removal of all forms of discrimination at work.

Other conventions of the ILO include provisions for maternity leave and maternity protection at work. In recent years, the ILO has also focused on the challenges posed by the digital economy and the growth of platform-based work. In 2024, the ILO released a report on achieving decent work in the platform economy, and has been developing a potential international standard on gig and platform workers, with discussions ongoing at the International Labour Conferences in 2025 and 2026. The ILO's concept of "decent work" — encompassing productive employment, fair income, workplace security, social protection, and the freedom to organize — continues to influence labour law reform in India and globally. India, as a founding member of the ILO, has ratified several of its key conventions and the four Labour Codes of 2025 reflect many of the ILO's core principles, including equal pay for equal work, maternity protection, occupational safety, and the extension of social security to all workers.

1.4 Main Labour Laws in India

The main labour laws in India include the following:

- Industrial Disputes Act 1947
- State Shops and Establishments Act
- Workmen's Compensation Act 1923
- Trade Unions Act 1926
- Industrial employment standing orders act 1946
- Payment of wages act 1936

In India there are 204-210 labour laws, out of which around 44 apply on a day-to-day basis. This was before the simplification of the laws in 2020.

Recently, the Indian government has come up with a new set of codes to simplify the labour laws. These are the following:

- Code of Wages, 2019
- Industrial Relations Code, 2020
- Occupational Safety, Health and Working Conditions Code 2020
- Code on Social Security, 2020

All four Labour Codes were officially brought into force on 21 November 2025, when the Government of India issued notifications in the Official Gazette implementing them nationwide. This marked a historic milestone in Indian labour law reform, as the Codes now replace 29 older central labour laws. However, the detailed central and state-level rules required for full implementation are still being finalized, with the Ministry of Labour and Employment releasing draft Central

Rules on 30 December 2025. Final rules are expected to be notified by April 2026, after which full compliance obligations will take effect across all states and union territories. During the transition period, the existing laws continue to apply in areas where state rules are not yet finalized.

1.5 Practical implications of important Indian labour laws

Some of the general characteristics of employment and other practical implications of important Indian labour laws are as follows:

The service conditions for employees have to be defined: This is as per the Industrial Employment Standing Orders Act. This is needed so that the employees can know what are the conditions of employment they are working with. These include things like working hours, paid leave, gratuity and so on. These are called standing orders. The standing orders act is applicable for 50+ employees in an establishment. The deputy labour commissioner is the certified authority for the purpose of ensuring this.

The standing orders give information including name of company, working hours, service condition, on what terms appointed/separated, how one must terminate employees, how workers get exit, misconduct and so on. There is a model standing order, which is to ensure that the companies cannot go beyond that model. If the standing order for a specific firm or establishment incorporates illegal terms, such as stating a bond or restricting the ex-employee from joining a competitor, they can be challenged.

However, in certain sectors and states, such as for the IT industry in Karnataka state, the government can pass an exemption for whole of the industry, saying standing orders act is not applicable to IT industry.

Definition of employee and management: This comes under the industrial employment standing orders act. As per the act, a supervisor or manager is one who has administrative powers, e.g. granting leave, reports, granting permissions etc, discharged on a continuous basis. If one occasionally has to discharge such powers during course of work, then he would be classified as a workman and not as a supervisor. It should be noted that standing orders act is only applicable to establishments having 50 or more employees.

Grievance mechanism: A grievance mechanism or procedure for redressal is required to be set in every establishment. The labour commissioner is the appellate authority for violations. There is a clause in standing order, not in letter and spirit, which is permission to prosecute. If such a mechanism is not present (apart from the sexual harassment mechanism which is also needed) it can be challenged.

Laws related to dispute related to termination or retrenchment: This comes under the Section 2(K) of Industrial disputes act. In case of termination or retrenchment, any individual can lay an industrial dispute. An industrial dispute is a dispute between an employee and a company. For things like denial of promotion etc, it can a collective dispute between the employees and the management of the firm, and therefore the employees need a union to fight for their behalf. A union need not be connected to a particular establishment or a particular industry. If there is presently no union for a specific industry or establishment, any general union such as CITU or AITUC or INTUC or Bharatiya Mazdoor Sangh can also support the petition of the worker.

The procedure in case of industrial disputes is as follows: the employees or the trade union approach the labour committee set up within the company, who first try to explore reconciliation between the employees and management via discussion. If the reconciliation is not fruitful, then the case goes to the labour commissioner, who gives his verdict and sends to government which sends it to the court whose jurisdiction falls in that area.

Often, employees do not approach courts fearing blacklisting from jobs in the future, however such blacklisting is also against the law. Every employee has a right to equality (article 14) and livelihood (article 21) - these are fundamental rights granted to all citizens by the Indian constitution. Article 19 of the constitution is the right to form associations.

Law in Special economic zones or SEZs: After liberalization, the government of India has set up many Special Economic Zones or SEZs, mainly to attract foreign investment. In SEZs also the labour laws are applicable. The main difference is that there may be specific exemptions, also the company needs to be informed in advance if the labour commissioner or other labour authorities come for an inspection of the premises at a specific pre-arranged time.

Forceful resignation: This comes under the Industrial Disputes act, under the section related to unfair labour practices, including acts of force or violence. Nobody can force the employee to resign. There are 5 schedules in Industrial Disputes act, which industries, which jurisdiction, which are conditions of service, which notices etc. These are applicable to every factory, establishment, individual. Even one employee.

Changes to terms and conditions of work: If the management of the establishment wish to change the mode of payment of wages, or some other condition of work such as PF, extend shift timings etc, they have to give the employee a 21 days notice. The employees can challenge the notice before the labour department, and the execution of the change is automatically stayed if such a challenge is made. Shift working and related matters come in the 4th schedule of the Industrial disputes act.

Unfair labour practices: If the employers interfere, refrain, or coerce the employees against joining or assisting a trade union, or threaten the employees with discharge or dismissal for trade union activities, the employees can file a complaint before the labour secretary of the state government.

Similarly, if the management forms a counter trade union, that is also an unfair labour practice. Similarly, discharging an employee for participating in a strike called by a trade union, also not allowed.

Layoff procedure: This is related to the Industrial Disputes Act section 2K. If more than 100 workmen are employed by the establishment, then prior permission must be taken before laying them off. If the number of employees is greater than 50 and less than 100, then 2 months of notice must be given. If it is less than 50 then full 100% wages has to be paid during the period of layoff.

Inspectors have to check whether the law of the land has been followed or not. In case of company closure, retrenchment, or layoff in an establishment of greater than 100 employees, the company has to apply to the secretary of labour department of the government for permission. If they take any other mode, the court will go deeper into the matter. If the labour commissioner files a complaint, the labour secretary will give relief to the employees. If employees are organized in a trade union, they can force the court to act. But many times, employees are weak and do not want to take risks. If company says stoppage of production (to justify termination of employees), but whole company is not closed and no wages are given, that too is illegal. These problems can only be solved collectively, not individually, by means of trade unions. Thus, trade unions perform an invaluable service of protection and support of the employees.

1.6 The 2025 Labour Code Implementation

On 21 November 2025, the Government of India issued official gazette notifications bringing all four Labour Codes into legal force simultaneously. This was widely described as the most significant reform of India's labour laws since independence. The four Codes: the Code on Wages 2019, the Industrial Relations Code 2020, the Code on Social Security 2020, and the Occupational Safety, Health and Working Conditions Code 2020, together replace 29 existing central labour laws, consolidating decades of fragmented legislation into a unified, modern framework.

The announcement came somewhat unexpectedly, as full implementation had been delayed for several years due to the need for states to publish their own implementing rules. Most states had pre-published draft rules by early 2025, and the central government decided to proceed with the notification to provide legal certainty. The Ministry of Labour and Employment clarified that during the transition period, the old laws would continue to apply in practice until the detailed central and state rules are finalized. Draft Central Rules were published on 30 December 2025, and the final rules are expected to be notified by April 2026.

The Codes introduce several important changes for workers. All workers are now entitled to minimum wages, salary credit by the 7th of every month, double wages for overtime, mandatory appointment letters, and free annual health check-ups. Fixed-term employees become eligible for gratuity after just one year of continuous service, a major change from the earlier requirement of five years. Women workers gain stronger rights including equal pay for equal work (now explicitly extended to all genders, including transgender persons), 26 weeks of paid maternity leave, and the right to work night shifts with appropriate safety measures. For the first time, gig and platform workers are formally recognized in India's labour law framework, with social security coverage and welfare fund contributions from aggregators. The Codes also introduce a facilitator-based inspection system, replacing the older enforcement-only model with a more compliance-friendly approach.

The implementation of the Codes has been welcomed as bringing India's labour ecosystem closer to global standards, though challenges remain in ensuring uniform compliance across 28 states and eight union territories, each of which must finalize their own rules.

1.7 Conclusion

In this chapter, we have introduced the main labour laws in India and some practical implications of the labour laws.

Chapter 2: Labour Protections in the Indian Constitution

In this chapter, we discuss the provisions related to work and labour in the constitution of India.

2.1 Introduction

Labour is part of the concurrent list in the Indian constitution i.e. it is both a central and state subject.

The constitution of India is quite progressive and contains a number of provisions related to improving labour conditions, removal of discrimination and equal rights for all workers. Labour related provisions come under sections on fundamental rights as well as directive principles of state policy in the Indian constitution.

Articles 14-16, 19(1)(c), 23-24, 38, and 41-43A of the Indian constitution are related to labour rights.

2.2 Articles related to labour in the Indian constitution

As per articles 14-16, everyone is equal before the law, the state should not discriminate between citizens and there is an equality of opportunity for employment under the state.

14. Equality before law The State shall not deny to any person equality before the law or the equal protection of the laws within the territory of India Prohibition of discrimination on grounds of religion, race, caste, sex or place of birth

15. Prohibition of discrimination on grounds of religion, race, caste, sex or place of birth (1) The State shall not discriminate against any citizen on grounds only of religion, race, caste, sex, place of birth or any of them

16. Equality of opportunity in matters of public employment (1) There shall be equality of opportunity for all citizens in matters relating to employment or appointment to any office under the State (2) No citizen shall, on grounds only of religion, race, caste, sex, descent, place of birth, residence or any of them, be ineligible for, or discriminated against in respect or, any employment or office under the State

As per the Article 19.1, part c of the Indian Constitution, there is the protection of citizens to form associations and trade unions.

A. ARTICLE 19: Protection of certain rights regarding freedom of speech etc: 1. All citizens shall have the right c) To form associations or unions.

As per Article 23 of the constitution, forced labour is forbidden.

23. Prohibition of traffic in human beings and forced labour: (1) Traffic in human beings and begar and other similar forms of forced labour are prohibited and any contravention of this provision shall be an offence punishable in accordance with law.

Article 24 prohibits child labour

24. Prohibition of employment of children in factories, etc No child below the age of fourteen years shall be employed to work in any factory or mine or engaged in any other hazardous employment Provided that nothing in this sub clause shall authorise the detention of any person beyond the maximum period prescribed by any law made by Parliament under sub clause (b) of clause (7); or such person is detained in accordance with the provisions of any law made by Parliament under sub clauses (a) and (b) of clause (7)

Article 38 makes it an aspiration of the Indian state to promote the welfare of the people.

38. State to secure a social order for the promotion of welfare of the people (1) The State shall strive to promote the welfare of the people by securing and protecting as effectively as it may a social order in which justice, social, economic and political, shall inform all the institutions of the national life (2) The State shall, in particular, strive to minimize the inequalities in income, and endeavor to eliminate inequalities in status, facilities and opportunities, not only amongst individuals but also amongst groups of people residing in different areas or engaged in different vocations

Article 39 provides for the right to livelihood and against exploitation

39. Certain principles of policy to be followed by the State: The State shall, in particular, direct its policy towards securing (a) that the citizens, men and women equally, have the right to an adequate means to livelihood; (b) that the ownership and control of the material resources of the community are so distributed as best to subserve the common good; (c) that the operation of the economic system does not result in the concentration of wealth and means of production to the common detriment; (d) that there is equal pay for equal work for both men and women; (e) that the health and strength of workers, men and women, and the tender age of children are not abused and that citizens are not forced by economic necessity to enter avocations unsuited to their age or strength; (f) that children are given opportunities and facilities to develop in a healthy manner and in conditions of freedom and dignity and that childhood and youth are protected against exploitation and against moral and material abandonment

Article 41 states that the state shall provide the right to work in certain cases.

41. Right to work, to education and to public assistance in certain cases The State shall, within the limits of its economic capacity and development, make effective provision for securing the right to work, to education and to public assistance in cases of unemployment, old age, sickness and disablement, and in other cases of undeserved want

Article 42 provides for just and humane conditions of work and maternity relief

42. Provision for just and humane conditions of work and maternity relief The State shall make provision for securing just and humane conditions of work and for maternity relief

Article 43 provides for a living wage and conditions of work.

43. Living wage, etc, for workers The State shall endeavour to secure, by suitable legislation or economic organisation or in any

other way, to all workers, agricultural, industrial or otherwise, work, a living wage, conditions of work ensuring a decent standard of life and full enjoyment of leisure and social and cultural opportunities and, in particular, the State shall endeavour to promote cottage industries on an individual or co operative basis in rural areas

2.3 Conclusion

In this chapter we have gone through various provisions related to work and labour present in the constitution of India. As we could see, the constitution is very progressive and provides for just and equal and fair conditions of work for all.

Chapter 3: Industrial Disputes Act

In this chapter we discuss the industrial disputes act 1947, which is one of the major labour laws of India for the organized sector and related to industrial disputes and strikes and the ways to resolve them.

THE INDUSTRIAL DISPUTES ACT, 1947

[14 OF 1947]

[11th March, 1947]

An Act to make provision for the investigation and settlement of industrial disputes, and for certain other purposes.

WHEREAS it is expedient to make provision for the investigation and settlement of industrial disputes, and for certain other purposes hereinafter appearing;

It is hereby enacted as follows:

CHAPTER-I
PRELIMINARY

1. Short title, extent and commencement.- (1) This Act may be called The Industrial Disputes Act, 1947.

[1][(2) It extends to the whole of India.]

[2][***]

(3) It shall come into force on the first day of April, 1947.

2. Definitions.- In this Act, unless there is anything repugnant in the subject or context,-

(a)   "appropriate Government" means-

(i)   in relation to any industrial dispute concerning [3][***] any industry carried on by or under the authority of the Central Government, [4][***] or by a railway company [5][or concerning any such controlled industry as may be specified in this behalf by the Central Government [6][***] or in relation to an industrial dispute concerning [7][8][9][10][a Dock Labour Board established under Section 5-A of the Dock Workers (Regulation of Employment) Act, 1948 or [11][the Industrial Finance Corporation of India Limited formed and registered under the Companies Act, 1956 (1 of 1956)] or the Employees State Insurance Corporation established under Section 3 of the Employees State Insurance Act, 1948 (34 of 1948),

---

1   Subs by Act No. 36 of 1956, sec. 2, for sub-section (2) (w.e.f. 29-8-1956).
2   Proviso omitted by Act 51 of 1970, sec. 2 and Sch. (w.e.f. 1-9-1971).
3   Certain words and figures ins. by Act 10 of 1963, S.47 and Sch.II, Pt. II have been omitted by Act 36 of 1964, S.2 (w.e.f. 19.12.1964)

Figure: First Page of the Industrial Disputes Act 1947

3.1 Introduction to the Industrial Disputes Act

The industrial disputes act 1947 was an act that consolidated the law in India for resolving industrial disputes, such as strikes and so on. It was focused mainly in the organized sectors of industry, comprising industries with regular employees with fixed work schedules and often which had trade unions among the employees, however it also covers contract employees.

The objective of this act was to secure a peaceful work environment. It also covered the compensation to workers who were laid off through retrenchment.

It was replaced by the Industrial Relations Code in 2020.

3.2 Summary of the Industrial Disputes Act

The Industrial Disputes Act provides for resolution and settlement of industrial disputes between the employees and the employers in a number of ways. It also provides for a mechanism for arbitration of disputes. This is mainly applicable for the organized sector, where the conditions of work are well defined, and the employees are permanent employees and not contract labour.

One of the mechanisms is mandating the establishment of a works committee in all industrial establishments with 100 or more employees. The committee is supposed to have equal number of workers and management.

Also, grievance redressal committees are required to be set up in all industrial establishments with 50 or more employees. It shall have not more than 6 members, with an equal number from management and workmen. Any worker can approach the committee to settle their grievance.

Some of the ways provided for the resolution of disputes are as follows:

- **Conciliation or mediation**: by setting up of a board of conciliation including a conciliation officer appointed by the government. The conciliation officer or board conducts conciliation proceedings to reach a reconciliation or settlement between the parties through mutual discussion and his judgment is binding.
- **Arbitration**: by voluntary referral of the dispute to a third-party arbitrator, whose arbitration award becomes binding on the parties.
- **Adjudication**: by setting up of an industrial tribunal or court of enquiry that conducts hearings on the dispute, and whose judgment is binding on the parties. Labour courts are also constituted under the act.

The act also stipulates that firms employing a certain minimum number of workers must take government permission in case of layoffs and retrenchments, as well as provide adequate compensation to the effected workers. It also covers unfair labour practices and seeks to prevent illegal strikes.

3.3 Conclusion

In this chapter we have briefly discussed the industrial disputes act, which provides for the means to settle industrial disputes between workers and employers.

Chapter 4: Industrial Employment Standing Orders Act

In this chapter we discuss the industrial employment standing orders act, which mandates employers to declare the conditions of work such as the working hours and the number of holidays.

4.1 Introduction to the standing orders act

Prior to the introduction of the standing orders act, often the conditions of work in Indian establishments were not well defined. The workers were subject to arbitrary rules and change of rules by the management, making them vulnerable to exploitation.

The standing orders act seeks to remedy this situation by mandating the employers to make the conditions of employment clear and known to all employees. This is applicable to all firms except those that have been defined as specifically exempt by the government in an official gazette.

It applies to the whole of India, although it has a few state-specific amendments such as those for Maharashtra and Karnataka. It applies to industrial establishments where a hundred or more workers were employed any day out of the preceding year. However, the act is not applicable for certain services such as the civil service and defence services.

THE INDUSTRIAL EMPLOYMENT (STANDING ORDERS) ACT, 1946

ACT NO. 20 OF 1946[1]

[23rd April, 1946.]

An Act to require employers in industrial establishments formally to define conditions of employment under them.

WHEREAS it is expedient to require employers in industrial establishments to define with sufficient precision the conditions of employment under them and to make the said conditions known to workmen employed by them;

It is hereby enacted as follows:—

STATE AMENDMENT

Maharashtra

Amendment of long title of Act XX of 1946.—In the Industrial Employment (Standing Orders) Act, 1946 (hereinafter referred to as "the said Act") for the long title the following shall be substituted, namely:—

"An Act to provide for defining with sufficient precision certain conditions of employment in industrial establishment in the State of Bombay."

[*Vide* Bombay Act XXI of 1958, s. 2]

Amendment of preamble of Act XX of 1946.—In the preamble of the said Act, for the portion beginning with the words "to require" and ending with the words "by them", the words "to provide for defining with sufficient precision certain conditions of employment in industrial establishment in the State of Bombay, and for certain other matters" shall be substituted.

[*Vide* Bombay Act XXI of 1958, s. 3]

1. Short title, extent and application.—(*1*) This Act may be called the Industrial Employment (Standing Orders) Act, 1946.

(*2*) It extends to[2][the whole of India [3]***].

[4][(*3*) It applies to every industrial establishment wherein one hundred or more workmen are employed, or were employed on any day of the preceding twelve months:

Provided that the appropriate Government may, after giving not less than two months' notice of its intention so to do, by notification in the Official Gazette, apply the provisions of this Act to any industrial establishment employing such number of persons less than one hundred as may be specified in the notification.

Figure: First Page of the Standing Orders Act 1946

4.2 What are standing orders

Standing orders include the following:

- Classification of workmen as permanent or temporary workers or apprentices etc
- Manner for informing the workers of details related to their work and salary
- Conditions of work related to attendance and late coming, shift working, leaves and how to apply for

leaves
- Entering the company premises by certain gates and the liability to search for the employees
- Rights and liabilities
- Termination or suspension of workers and the required notice to be given
- How workers can seek redressal if they are terminated or subject to unfair treatment

4.3 Certification and posting of standing orders

The standing orders act holds that the standing orders for any establishment need to be certifiable, as long as they are in conformity with the standing orders act. Workers or trade unions can raise objections to any of the conditions, and the certifying officer can adjudicate on the fairness or reasonableness of any of the standing orders. Their judgments shall be binding on the parties, however they can be appealed at an appellate authority. The certification and appellate authorities have the power of a civil court.

Once they are certified, the standing orders shall be posted in the establishment in English on special notice boards near the entrance where they can be visible to all the workers.

The act also provides for the case where a worker has been suspended pending an investigation, in which case for the first 90 days of suspension 50 percent of the usual salary shall be paid to the worker and 75 percent for the remaining days if the delay is not caused by the worker.

4.4 Conclusion

In this chapter we have discussed the standing orders act, that mandate the employer to fix and clearly display to all employees the conditions of work.

Chapter 5: Trade Unions Act

In this chapter we discuss the trade unions act 1926, which was one of the early labour laws established in British India and which still holds today with some modifications. The act covers the establishment, registration, rights and liabilities and working of trade unions in India.

THE TRADE UNIONS ACT, 1926

ACT NO. 16 OF 1926[1]

[*25th March, 1926.*]

An Act to provide for the registration of Trade Unions and in certain respects to define the law relating to registered Trade Unions [2]***.

WHEREAS it is expedient to provide for the registration of Trade Unions and in certain respects to define the law relating to registered Trade Unions [2]***; It is hereby enacted as follows:—

CHAPTER I

PRELIMINARY

1. Short title, extent and commencement.—(*1*) This Act may be called the [3]*** Trade Unions Act, 1926.

[4][(*2*) It extends to the whole of India [5]***.]

(*3*) It shall come into force on such date[6] as the Central Government may, by notification in the Official Gazette, appoint.

2. Definitions.—In this Act, [7]["the appropriate Government" means, in relation to Trade Unions whose objects are not confined to one State, the Central Government, and in relation to other Trade Unions, the State Government, and] unless there is anything repugnant in the subject or context,—

(*a*) "executive" means the body, by whatever name called, to which the management of the affairs of a Trade Union is entrusted;

(*b*) "[8][office-bearer]", in the case of a Trade Union, includes any member of the executive thereof, but does not include an auditor;

(*c*) "prescribed" means prescribed by regulations made under this Act;

(*d*) "registered office" means that office of a Trade Union which is registered under this Act as the head office thereof;

(*e*) "registered Trade Union" means a Trade Union registered under this Act;

[9][(*f*) "Registrar" means—

(*i*) a Registrar of Trade Unions appointed by the appropriate Government under section 3, and includes any Additional or Deputy Registrar of Trade Unions; and

(*ii*) in relation to any Trade Union, the Registrar appointed for the State in which

Figure: First Page of the Trade Unions Act 1946

5.1 Introduction and history of trade unions in India

A trade union is an organized group of workers who represent all the workers in the establishment and strive to fight for better pay and conditions of work. They are a means of collective bargaining by the workers in case of conditions of work and pay and also for calling industrial action or strikes in case their demands are not met by the employers.

Trade unions are covered and regulated by the trade unions act. Historically, trade unions have been responsible for a number of improvements in working conditions such as 8 hours work a day, holidays, minimum wages and so on.

All over the world, with the advent of the industrial age trade unions started in different industries around the 19th century. Being one of the first industrialized powers, Britain was the one of the first places where trade unions arose. Since India was ruled by Britain and had a number of industries such as cotton mills in the big cities such as Bombay, Calcutta and Madras, trade unions started in India as well in the latter half of the 19th century. The first trade union in India is generally known to be Bombay Mill-Hands Association which was founded by N.M. Lokhande in 1890.

However due to the discontent caused by the first world war and the Russian revolution that inspired workers all over the world, they rose rapidly after the first world war. The first registered union was the Madras Labour union in 1918 founded by BP Wadia. The All India Trade Union Congress or AITUC was set up in 1920. The Trade Unions Act was brought in 1926 to control and monitor the trade unions. There are a number of all India trade unions currently such as CITU (Centre of Indian Trade Unions), AITUC (All India Trade Union Congress), INTUC (Indian National Trade Union Congress), Bharatiya Mazdoor Sangh and so on, many of them affiliated to political parties in India. There are also sector specific unions such as All India Bank Employees Association and All India Railwaymen's Federation.

Figure: Logos of some of the trade unions in India.

After the liberalization of the Indian economy in the 1990s, the trade union membership has been declining, especially in the new industries such as IT. However, they still have substantial membership in traditional sectors such as banking, railways, electricity and communications.

5.2 Summary of the Trade Unions Act

The trade unions act contains sections related to registration of a trade union in front of a registrar appointed by the government.

A form must be submitted in a proper format, along with documents showing the list of office bearers, rules of the trade union, a list of assets and liabilities of the trade union, address of the registered office and other documents.

There must be a minimum number of employees in order to register a trade union, which is at least 10% of the strength of the establishment or 100 members, whichever is less, out of which at least 7 should be in active employment of the establishment at the time of registration. A few other regulations also need to be met before the trade union registration is approved and the certificate of registration given.

The rules of the trade union include the name of the trade union, the object of establishment, objects on which the trade union funds can be spent such as salaries to office bearers and costs of legal suits, including a separate fund for supporting political parties, conditions under which the members are entitled to benefit from the rules, procedure of amendment, audit of the funds and inspection of the books, and finally the manner of dissolution of the trade union.

The act contains provisions about disqualification and change of office bearers, as well as the procedure for dissolution of a trade union. It has sections about regulations of trade unions, including the power to make regulations and publication of the regulations. It has provision of penalties levied on the trade union in case of not submitting their returns to the registrar including an audit report with assets and liabilities or supplying false information.

FORM A

Application for Registration of Trade Union

Dated the ....day of ....19..............

1-   We hereby apply for the registration of a Trade Union under the name of

2-   The Address of the head office of the Union is

3-   The Union came in the existence on the ....day of ....19.....

4-   The Union is a Union of employers (Workers engaged in the industry of profession).

5-   The particulars required by section 5 (1) (c) of the Indian Trade Union Act. 1926.

6-   The Particulars given in Schedule II show the provision made in the rules for the matters detailed in section 6 of the Indian Trade Union Act, 1926.

7-   (To be struck out in the case of unions which have not been in existence for one year before the date of application. The particular required by section 5 (2) of the Indian Trade Union Act, 1926, are given in Schedule III.*

8.   We have been duly authorized to make this application.

	Signature	Occupation	Address
Signed	1		
	2		
	3		
	4		
	5		
	6		
	7		

To the Registrar of Central Trade Unions , Delhi

*   *State here whether the authority was given by a resolution of a general meeting of the Union, if not, in what other way it was given.*

Figure: Sample application for the registration of a trade union. This is accompanied with a list of officers, rules and statement of assets and liabilities of the trade union and a few other documents.

5.3 Conclusion

In this chapter we have discussed the trade unions act, which is mainly for the purpose of registering and regulating trade unions, which are instruments of collective bargaining and welfare of the employees.

Chapter 6: Payment of Wages Act, Employees Compensation Act and Minimum Wages Act

In this chapter we discuss the a few laws related to payment of wages in India. These include the payment of wages act 1936, the employees compensation act 1923 and the minimum wages act 1948. The objective of these acts is to ensure a fair and timely payment of wages to the workers, and also compensation in case of injuries sustained.

6.1 Employees Compensation Act 1923

The Employees Compensation Act, also called Workmen's Compensation Act, provides for the payment of compensation to employees or their dependents or next of kin. The compensation is to be paid in case of an accident, that causes death or serious injuries. The injuries should be sustained during the course of their work and while performing their work duties, usually on the employer's premises. The injuries covered under the act should be for more than three days.

Occupational diseases such as those arising out of exposure to harmful chemicals during their course of work are also covered under the act.

However, the employer is not liable to pay compensation if the injury was sustained when the employee was drunk or on drugs, or had wilfully disobeyed rules or procedures for their own safety, or wilfully removed any safety equipment.

The amount of compensation to be paid depends partly on whether the employee too had a contributory negligence in causing the injuries.

In case of the employee's death, an amount up to 50% of the employee's monthly wages multiplied by a factor is payable. In case of permanent partial or total disablement, 60% of the wages is payable.

In case the payment of compensation is not made by the employer, the employee may raise a dispute with the labour office or the labour comissioner.

6.2 Payment of Wages act 1936

This act provides for the timely payment of the employee's wages on or before the 7th of each month, if the number of workers is less than 1000, or 10th of each month otherwise. The payment of wages should be made in notes or coins, and by cheque if the employee consents. No wage period should exceed one month.

It also provides for protection against unauthorized deduction to wages made by the employer. Authorized deductions include fines, absence from duty, deductions for services given by the employer, damage or loss, recovery of loan etc and any deduction that is not authorized is considered as an unauthorized deduction for which the employee may raise a dispute through their union or by approaching the labour office.

6.3 Minimum Wages Act 1948

This act provides for fixing of rates of minimum wages to skilled and unskilled workers of various occupations, on a per day basis. The minimum wage includes the basic as well as the variable dearness allowance component.

The fixing of minimum wage is based on the cost of living and can be fixed for an entire state or an entire class of employment. State and central governments have the power to fix and change the minimum wages as deemed necessary. If the employer does not pay the minimum wages, they would be liable to penalties.

6.4 Payment of Bonus Act 1965

This act applies to any establishment with more than 20 workers and mandates the employers to pay an annual bonus to eligible employees as a percentage of the salary. The eligible employees are those who are earning less than 21000 a month and have worked in the establishment for at least 30 days in the year. The minimum bonus is fixed at 8.33% or Rupees 100 and maximum at 20% of the salary during the year. The bonus is paid out of the gross profits of the employer, after deduction of taxes.

The government can appoint inspectors who can inspect the premises and the records to ensure the bonus and wages are being paid on a timely basis. In case of violations, the employers are liable for penalties including imprisonment or fines.

6.5 Conclusion

In this chapter we have discussed a few acts related to wages, bonus and compensation to be paid to the employees.

Chapter 7: Factories Act

In this chapter we discuss the Factories Act 1948, which provides safeguards to improve working conditions and protect the health and safety of employees working in factories, including measures for prevention of accidents.

THE FACTORIES ACT, 1948

ACT NO. 63 OF 1948[1]

[23*rd September,* 1948.]

An Act to consolidate and amend the law regulating labour in factories.

WHEREAS it is expedient to consolidate and amend the law regulating labour in factories;

It is hereby enacted as follows:—

CHAPTER I

PRELIMINARY

1. Short title, extent and commencement.—(*1*) This Act may be called the Factories Act, 1948.

[2][(*2*) It extends to the whole of India [3]***.]

(*3*) It shall come into force on the 1st day of April 1949.

2. Interpretation.—In this Act, unless there is anything repugnant in the subject or context,—

(*a*) "adult" means a person who has completed his eighteenth year of age;

(*b*) "adolescent" means a person who has completed his fifteenth year of age but has not completed his eighteenth year;

[4][(*bb*) "calendar year" means the period of twelve months beginning with the first day of January in any year;]

(*c*) "child" means a person who has not completed his fifteenth year of age;

[5][(*ca*) "competent person", in relation to any provision of this Act, means a person or an institution recognised as such by the Chief Inspector for the purposes of carrying out tests, examinations and inspections required to be done in a factory under the provisions of this Act having regard to—

(*i*) the qualifications and experience of the person and facilities available at his disposal; or

(*ii*) the qualifications and experience of the persons employed in such institution and facilities available therein,

with regard to the conduct of such tests, examinations and inspections, and more than one person or institution can be recognised as a competent person in relation to a factory;

(*cb*) "hazardous process" means any process or activity in relation to an industry specified in the First Schedule where, unless special care is taken, raw materials used therein or the intermediate or

Figure: First page of the Factories Act 1948

7.1 Introduction to the factories act

The factories act provides for a wide array of benefits and protections related to the employees' health and safety. It is applicable to any premises with 10 or more workers. The owner of the business, called the occupier, is responsible for ensuring the provisions related to safety and welfare under the act, with penalties defined if they fail to comply. The overall intention is to enhance the health and safety of the employees and to make the workplace more pleasant.

7.2 Summary of the factories act

As per the factories act, no adult worker can work more than 48 hours a week or 9 hours a day without payment of overtime wages. Similarly, if the workers are deprived of their statutory holidays, they would be given compensatory holidays or paid for the same.

It provides for the employer to maintain cleanliness in the factory premises, timely disposal of wastes and effluents. maintenance of a good ventilation, temperature and humidification via means such as air circulation, prevention of dust and fumes that can cause injury to the workers, prevention of overcrowding, adequate lighting, provision of latrines, urinals and spittoons.

The act also has some safety related mandates, which include fencing of machinery, prohibition of employment of young inexperienced people on dangerous machines without adequate instruction given, casing of new machinery, and provision of striking gear and devices to cut power immediately in case of a safety incident. It also covers disclosure and inspection of hazardous processes.

For the welfare of workers in the factory, the act provides for facilities such as canteens, facilities for sitting, storing and drying clothing, first aid boxes, rest rooms and lunch-rooms with drinking water provision and creches for taking care of young children in establishments where more than 30 women workers are employed.

7.3 Conclusion

In this chapter we have gone through the provisions of the factories act, which is intended to ensure basic health and safety related measures for people working in factories.

Chapter 8: Code of Wages 2019

In this chapter we discuss the Code of Wages 2019, which is one of the four codes brought by the Indian government to simplify the labour laws in India. This code mainly deals with laws related to wages and salaries, overtime, bonus and minimum wages etc.

Figure: First page of the Code of Wages 2019

8.1 Introduction to the Code of Wages

The Code of Wages was brought in 2019 by the current Indian government. The idea was to simplify and modernize the numerous laws related to labour and working conditions, balance the interests of employers and employees and to consolidate all the labour laws into four main codes namely the code of wages, code of social security, code of occupational safety, health and working conditions and code of industrial relations code.

The Code of wages replaces the previous existing laws: Payment of Wages Act 1936, the Minimum Wages Act 1948, the Payment of Bonus Act 1965 and the Equal Remuneration Act 1976.

8.2 Summary of the code of wages

The wages includes basic pay, dearness allowance and retention allowance and excludes components such as bonus, employer provided accommodation, PF and pension contributions, HRA, gratuity etc. All these components should not exceed 50% of the total.

Under this code, the central government sets a national floor rate for wages, taking into account living standards. The minimum wages for any state must be higher than the floor wage, and can be set for time work such as daily, monthly etc and take into consideration the workers' skills and other factors. Employers must pay their workers at least the minimum wages. The minimum wage rates must be revised every five years.

The working hours in a working day are fixed by the central or state governments. A rest day must be provided every seven days and workers must be paid at the overtime rate, which must be at least double the normal rate, if working hours are exceeded or if they are asked to work on the rest day.

Wages can be paid by any of the following modes: cash, cheque, credit to the bank or electronic mode. Wages can only be deducted by the employer in case of fines or losses or absence from duty or recovery of advances, and the deductions cannot exceed 50% of the total wages.

All employees in establishments with more than 20 people with at least 30 days of work, with wages less than a minimum amount are entitled to a bonus not less than 8.33% and not more than 20% of the annual wages. The bonus shall be taken from the surplus taken from the gross profits.

Gender discrimination in payment of wages is prohibited and equal renumeration for the same work is mandated. Advisory boards shall be set up by central and state governments for increasing employment for women.

Authorities shall be appointed by the government to hear claims related to the code and aim to settle them within three months. The code contains penalties for employers who violate the code, including imprisonment for 3 months and fines of Rupees 1 lakh. Inspectors shall be appointed by the government for web based inspection that companies are complying with the code.

Central and state rules related to the code of wages have been drafted as well.

8.3 Conclusion

In this chapter we have discussed the code of wages, that is a recent law to consolidate multiple wage related laws.

Chapter 9: Occupational Safety, Health and Working Conditions Code 2020

In this chapter we discuss the Occupational Health safety and working conditions code 2020, also called OHS code which is one of the four new codes brought by the Indian government to reform and simplify the labour laws.

9.1 Introduction to the OHS Code 2020

The OHS code consolidates various existing laws related to health and safety of workers employed in various occupations. It replaces various existing acts including the Contract Labour (Regulation and Abolition) Act 1970, Mines Act 1952, Factories Act 1948 and inter state migrant workers act 1979.

It has various provisions for health and safety and welfare of employees at the workplace.

Figure: First page of the OHS Code 2020

9.2 Summary of the OHS code

The OHS code is applicable for all premises with at least 20 employees for factories with power and 40 without power. It fixes the maximum work daily to 8 hours and work for only 6 days a week, with minimum leaves per year. It includes a provision for leave encashments as well.

It also includes and provides for contract labour, where the contractor is present and the principal employer is different from the employer of the workers, and inter-state migrant workers. It allows women to be employed during the night hours from 7 pm to 6 am subject to consent and provisions being made for their safety. It ensures that no charge is levied for health and safety measures including annual health check-ups and medical tests. It also provides for the constitution of a National Occupational Safety and Health Advisory Board and similar boards at the state level.

The code includes a number of health and safety measures similar to those defined in the factories act. These include measures to make a safe working environment with reduced accidents and measures to keep the workplace free from hazards including hazardous waste. It includes provision of separate washing facilities for male and female employees, separate bathing places and locker rooms, creche facilities, canteens, sitting arrangements for workers, first aid facilities, cleanliness and hygiene at the workplace, provision of drinking water, adequate lighting, and avoidance of overcrowding. It also reduces the burden on employers by having only one common license and one electronic registration instead of multiple registrations, and one consolidated return to be filed.

9.3 Conclusion

In this chapter we have briefly discussed the OHS code that consolidates and replaces the laws related to employees' health and safety.

Chapter 10: Code on Social Security 2020

In this chapter we discuss the Code on Social Security 2020, which is one of the four new codes brought by the Indian government to reform and simplify the labour laws. It consolidates the laws related to the social security benefits for all employees in the organized and unorganized sectors.

Figure: First page of the Code on Social Security 2020

10.1 Introduction to the code on Social Security

The code on social security aims to consolidate existing laws and also to extend the social security benefits to all employees including unorganized sector employees such as construction workers, gig workers, platform workers and migrant workers. It focuses on existing schemes such as provident fund and EPF and insurance for the employees.

It consolidates and replaces multiple existing acts related to social security, including the Employees' Compensation Act 1923, Employees' State Insurance Act 1948, Employees' Provident Funds and Miscellaneous Provisions Act 1952, Employment Exchanges (Compulsory Notification of Vacancies) Act 1959, Maternity Benefit Act 1961, Payment of Gratuity Act 1972, and Unorganised Workers' Social Security Act 2008.

10.2 Summary of the code on social security

As per the social security code, gig workers and other workers are all eligible for life insurance and disability insurance, maternity benefits, pension benefits, provident fund, and so on. Fixed term contract workers are now eligible for gratuity in addition to permanent employees, in case of events such as retirement, resignation and death. Previously, the contract workers and workers in the unorganized sector were largely left uncovered.

Existing wage ceilings for coverage are now removed. It also includes penalties on the employers in case of non-compliance. All records and returns are to be maintained electronically. Inspectors cum facilitators are appointed to inspect the returns and also provide guidance to the employers regarding compliance.

The social security benefits such as EPF, EPS and EDLI are delivered using existing bodies such as central and state level social security boards.

Employees Provident Fund or EPF provisions are applicable to establishments with more than 20 employees. The employer is liable to contribute 10% of the wages payable to each employee to the provident fund, with an equal contribution or more being paid by the employee. The employer must maintain a provident fund account for the same.

Employees State Insurance Corporation or ESIC provisions are applicable for establishments with 10 or more people, including for those with hazardous or life-threatening occupations with even one employee and plantation employees. All employees shall be insured and a separate fund shall be maintained, the money being used to pay for medical treatment and other benefits as needed.

The code also includes provisions for payment of gratuities, maternity benefits, employees compensation and so on.

10.3 Gig and Platform Workers under the Social Security Code

One of the most significant and forward-looking aspects of the Code on Social Security 2020 is its inclusion of gig workers and platform workers within the formal social security framework for the first time in India's history. India has one of the world's largest and fastest-growing gig economies, with millions of workers engaged in platform-based services such as food delivery (Zomato, Swiggy), ride-hailing (Ola, Uber), e-commerce logistics, and quick commerce (Blinkit, Zepto). NITI Aayog estimated over 7.7 million gig workers as of 2020, with the number growing rapidly since.

The Code formally defines gig workers, platform workers, and aggregators in law. A gig worker is defined as a person who performs work or participates in a work arrangement outside of a traditional employer-employee relationship. A platform worker performs work based on online software apps or digital platforms. An aggregator is a digital intermediary or market place which uses IT or a digital interface to connect buyers and sellers of goods or services.

Under the Code, aggregators are required to contribute between 1% and 2% of their annual turnover (capped at 5% of the total amount payable to gig and platform workers) to a dedicated Social Security Fund. This fund finances welfare schemes covering life and disability insurance, accident insurance, health and maternity benefits, old age protection, and other benefits notified by the government. Gig workers can self-register on the e-Shram portal, a national database for unorganized workers, and receive an Aadhaar-linked Universal Account Number (UAN) that ensures portability of benefits when they move between states or between different platforms. The Union Budget 2025-26 also announced that registered gig workers would receive identity cards and healthcare coverage under the PM Jan Arogya Yojana scheme.

Several states have gone further than the central framework in protecting gig workers. Rajasthan was the first state to pass a dedicated law, the Rajasthan Platform-Based Gig Workers (Registration and Welfare) Act, in July 2023. Karnataka passed the Karnataka Platform-Based Gig Workers (Social Security and Welfare) Act in August 2025, which establishes a Welfare Board, creates a dedicated fund financed by a fee on each platform transaction, mandates written reasons for worker deactivation, and requires algorithmic transparency from platforms. Bihar and Jharkhand also passed similar laws in August 2025. In a landmark 2024 order, the Karnataka High Court upheld the applicability of the Prevention of Sexual Harassment (POSH) Act to gig workers, affirming that platform aggregators have an obligation to ensure a safe working environment for them.

Internationally, the classification and protection of gig workers is a contested issue. In the United Kingdom, the Supreme Court ruled that Uber drivers are "workers" entitled to minimum wage and holiday pay. France's Court of Cassation similarly found that an Uber driver had an employment relationship with the platform. The International Labour Organization has been developing a framework for decent work in the platform economy, which may lead to an international standard in coming years. India's approach, providing social security without formally classifying gig workers as employees, represents a middle path that aims to balance flexibility for platforms with protections for workers.

10.4 Conclusion

In this chapter we have gone through the code on social security, which consolidates, simplifies and replaces existing laws related to PF, gratuity and other related benefits.

Chapter 11: Industrial Relations Code 2020

———

In this chapter we discuss the Industrial Relations Code 2020, which is one of the four new codes brought by the Indian government to reform and simplify the labour laws. It reforms existing laws related to trade unions, conditions of employment and industrial disputes.

MINISTRY OF LAW AND JUSTICE
(Legislative Department)

New Delhi, the 29th September, 2020/Asvina 7, 1942 (Saka)

The following Act of Parliament received the assent of the President on the 28th September, 2020 and is hereby published for general information:—

THE INDUSTRIAL RELATIONS CODE, 2020

No. 35 of 2020

[28th September, 2020.]

An Act to consolidate and amend the laws relating to Trade Unions, conditions of employment in industrial establishment or undertaking, investigation and settlement of industrial disputes and for matters connected therewith or incidental thereto.

Be it enacted by Parliament in the Seventy-first Year of the Republic of India as follows:—

CHAPTER I

PRELIMINARY

1. (*1*) This Act may be called the Industrial Relations Code, 2020.

(*2*) It shall extend to the whole of India.

(*3*) It shall come into force on such date as the Central Government may, by notification in the Official Gazette appoint; and different dates may be appointed for different provisions of this Code and any reference in any such provision to the commencement of this Code shall be construed as a reference to the coming into force of that provision.

Figure: First page of the Industrial Relations Code 2020

11.1 Introduction to the Industrial Relations Code

The Industrial Relations code 2020 replaces three important existing laws: the Trade Unions Act 1926, Industrial Employment (Standing Orders) Act 1946 and Industrial Disputes Act 1947.

It reforms the existing laws related to conditions of employment and industrial disputes.

11.2 Summary of the Industrial Relations Code 2020

The industrial relations code introduces more conditions for a legal strike by workers and increases the threshold for layoffs and firings without getting government permission to 300 workers from the existing 100. It thus focuses on providing more flexibility to employers to hire and fire workers.

It provides a broader framework for workers to form unions. It introduces new concepts for recognition of trade unions as follows: if there is only a single union in a company it is recognized as the sole trade union. In case of multiple unions, the one with 51% workers is recognized. If no union has 51% workers, the employer forms a negotiating council with representatives of the registered trade unions.

It amends the definition of strike to mass casual leave. If 50% or more employees go on casual leave, then it is treated as a strike. However, workers cannot go on a strike without 14 days notice. No employer can lock out any employees without at least 14 days notice. Lockouts and strikes are prohibited after 7 days of arbitration, or during the period of an arbitration award or settlement award. The government has the power to postpone enforcement of the tribunal awards.

Complaint redressal committees are required for establishments with more than 20 employees, with not exceeding 10 members and equal representation from the employees and management side.

Standing orders are required for establishments with 300 or more employees.

The code provides for a reskilling fund for laid off employees, which is used to pay the last 15 days salary for the laid off worker within 45 days of the dismissal. 50% of the basic wages and dearness allowance should be paid if an employee is laid off. In case of retrenchment, one months' notice or equivalent salary must be given and 15 days salary for each year of continuous service completed must be paid.

11.3 Conclusion

In this chapter, we have discussed the industrial relations code. Its objective is to reform the existing laws related to industrial relations and provide for harmonious relations between the employers and employees.

Chapter 12: Remedies for Unfair Dismissal from a Job

In this chapter, we discuss the actions that an employee might take in case of unfair dismissal or retrenchment from their job by the employer.

12.1 Unfair Dismissal

Unfair dismissal or termination of employment is where an employer terminates the employment of an employee without giving a strong and valid reason.

As per the **Industrial Relations Code 2020**, termination of employment for any reason other than disciplinary action comes under retrenchment. This requires a month's written notice period on part of the employer, along with 15 days of average pay as compensation for every year of active service with that employer.

Some employers, to avoid paying the compensation and other legal steps, try to force the employees to resign. However, forced resignation is not valid or legal as per the labour laws in India.

12.2 Retrenchments in the Industrial Relations Code 2020

The code states the following provisions related to layoffs and retrenchments:

"retrenchment" means the termination by the employer of the service of a worker for any reason whatsoever, otherwise than as a punishment inflicted by way of disciplinary action,

No worker employed in any industry who has been in continuous service for not less than one year under an employer shall be retrenched by that employer until—

(a) the worker has been given one month's notice in writing indicating the reasons for retrenchment and the period of notice has expired, or the worker has been paid in lieu of such notice, wages for the period of the notice;

(b) the worker has been paid, at the time of retrenchment, compensation which shall be equivalent to fifteen days' average pay, or average pay of such days as may be notified by the appropriate Government, for every completed year of continuous service or any part thereof in excess of six months; and

(c) notice in such manner as may be prescribed is served on the appropriate Government or such authority as may be specified by the appropriate Government by notification.

67. Whenever a worker (other than a badli worker or a casual worker) whose name is borne on the muster rolls of an industrial establishment and who has completed not less than one year of continuous service under an employer is laid-off, whether continuously or intermittently, he shall be paid by the employer for all days during which he is so laid-off, except for such weekly holidays as may intervene, compensation which shall be equal to fifty per cent. of the total of the basic wages and dearness allowance that would have been payable to him had he not been so laid-off:

Provided that if during any period of twelve months, a worker is so laid-off for more than forty-five days, no such compensation shall be payable in respect of any period of the lay-off after the expiry of the first forty-five days, if there is an agreement to that effect between the worker and the employer:

Provided further that it shall be lawful for the employer in any case falling within the foregoing proviso to retrench the worker in accordance with the provisions contained in section 70 at any time after the expiry of the first forty-five days of the lay-off and when he does so, any compensation paid to the worker for having been laid-off during the preceding twelve months may be set off against the compensation payable for retrenchment.

12.3 Remedies in case of unfair dismissal

In case a number of employees have been forced to resign, the group of employees can together approach the labour boards or labour commissioner. They can also approach the labour unions, if they exist, for assistance and advice. They can also approach the courts.

In addition, if the employee feels they have been discriminated in their termination from work, they can approach the courts for compensation for discrimination as well. Discrimination at work, particularly gender discrimination in terms of wages, is against the labour laws.

12.4 Conclusion

In this chapter we have discussed the laws related to unfair dismissal and what are the remedies available for employees retrenched or unfairly dismissed.

Chapter 13: Laws Related to Sexual Harassment at Work

In this chapter we discuss the laws related to sexual harassment at work. Since sexual harassment at work is a major issue especially for the well-being of female employees and creating a hostile work environment, it has been dealt with in the labour laws.

THE SEXUAL HARASSMENT OF WOMEN AT WORKPLACE
(PREVENTION, PROHIBITION AND REDRESSAL) ACT, 2013

ACT NO. 14 OF 2013

[22nd April, 2013]

An Act to provide protection against sexual harassment of women at workplace and for the prevention and redressal of complaints of sexual harassment and for matters connected therewith or incidental thereto.

WHEREAS sexual harassment results in violation of the fundamental rights of a woman to equality under articles 14 and 15 of the Constitution of India and her right to life and to live with dignity under article 21 of the Constitution and right to practice any profession or to carry on any occupation, trade or business with includes a right to a safe environment free from sexual harassment;

AND WHEREAS the protection against sexual harassment and the right to work with dignity are universally recognised human rights by international conventions and instruments such as Convention on the Elimination of all Forms of Discrimination against Women, which has been ratified on the 25th June, 1993 by the Government of India;

AND WHEREAS it is expedient to make provisions for giving effect to the said Convention for protection of women against sexual harassment at workplace.

BE it enacted by Parliament in the Sixty-fourth Year of the Republic of India as follows: —

CHAPTER I

PRELIMINARY

1. Short title, extent and commencement.—(*1*) This Act may be called the Sexual Harassment of Women at Workplace (Prevention, Prohibition and Redressal) Act, 2013.

(*2*) It extends to the whole of India.

(*3*) It shall come into force on such date[1] as the Central Government may, by notification in the Official Gazette, appoint.

2. Definitions.—In this Act, unless the context otherwise requires, —

(*a*) "aggrieved woman" means—

(*i*) in relation to a workplace, a woman, of any age whether employed or not, who alleges to have been subjected to any act of sexual harassment by the respondent;

(*ii*) in relation to dwelling place or house, a woman of any age who is employed in such a dwelling place or house;

(*b*) "appropriate Government" means—

(*i*) in relation to a workplace which is established, owned, controlled or wholly or substantially financed by funds provided directly or indirectly—

(*A*) by the Central Government or the Union territory administration, the Central Government;

Figure: First page of the Sexual Harassment Act 2013

13.1 Introduction to the Sexual Harassment of Women at Workplace Act

The Sexual Harassment of Women at Workplace (Prevention, Prohibition and Redressal) Act was passed in 2013 by the government. It provides for an environment which ensures the women's right to workplace equality and freedom from sexual harassment.

13.2 Summary of the Sexual Harassment Act

Sexual harassment includes unwanted and unwelcome acts towards women including physical contact and advances, demands or requests for sexual favours, making sexually coloured remarks, showing pornography or any other unwelcome physical, verbal or non-verbal conduct of sexual nature.

If a women employee is promised preferential treatment or threatened with detrimental treatment conditional on the giving of sexual favours, it constitutes sexual harassment.

The company shall constitute an internal complaints committee, consisting of a woman presiding officer from the management and one or two male or female employees, for investigation of complaints. It may also file a local committee.

Any woman may approach the committee with her complaint with details in writing within three months of the incident. The committee may on the request of the woman attempt to settle the dispute through conciliation, failing which they will proceed with their inquiry. The committee can forward the complaint to the police if it deems fit, such as if the woman states the respondent is not complying with the terms and conditions of the settlement.

The complaints committee shall have the same powers as are vested in a civil court in relation to summoning and examining witnesses under oath and examining evidence.

The remedies available are various types of relief including transfer of the victim or respondent to another workplace, granting of leave to the aggrieved women up to three months or other kinds of relief. They can also pay compensation for the loss and trauma as well as career opportunity loss and medical expenses, to the aggrieved woman. It may also restrain the respondent from reporting on the work performance of the aggrieved woman.

As per the law, the employer also has a responsibility for a harassment free and safe working environment at the workplace. To that end they may constitute Prevention of Sexual Harassment or POSH workshops or training programs for all employees, raise awareness of the internal committee, treat sexual harassment as misconduct under the service rules and report on the number of such cases filed and disposed. If the employer does not comply with the requirements, they can be punished including removal of their license to operate the business.

13.3 Conclusion

In this chapter we have discussed the prevention of sexual harassment act, which aims to make the workplace a safe working environment for women.

Chapter 14: Conclusion

Labour laws are important and vital to providing a safe working environment where the employees can have better productivity and realize their potential at work. They are conducive to a better and more productive workplace and the development of the nation.

The implementation of the four Labour Codes on 21 November 2025 marks a watershed moment for Indian labour law. For the first time since independence, workers across sectors — formal, informal, gig, contract, migrant, and platform-based — are brought under a single, modernized legal architecture. The consolidation of 29 old laws into four Codes addresses decades of fragmentation, overlap, and complexity that had made compliance difficult for employers and left many workers unprotected. The Codes strike a balance between worker welfare and ease of doing business, reflecting global trends in labour law reform while remaining sensitive to India's unique economic and social conditions.

Key highlights of the ongoing reform include the recognition of gig workers in law, portability of social security benefits through Aadhaar-linked accounts, gender-inclusive wage equality for all genders including transgender persons, strengthened protections for women working night shifts, gratuity entitlement for fixed-term employees after just one year of service, and a shift from punitive inspections to a facilitator-based compliance model. Internationally, India's labour law reforms align with standards promoted by the ILO, including the principles of decent work, social security for all, and non-discrimination at the workplace.

Challenges, however, remain. The detailed rules under the Codes are still being finalized at both the central and state levels, and employers and workers alike must navigate a transition period where old laws continue to apply in some areas. States such as West Bengal and a few union territories have been slower to align their rules. The gig economy continues to grow rapidly, and questions around worker classification, algorithmic management, and the balance between flexibility and protection are evolving issues that future legislation will need to address. The Supreme Court of India has also been seized with challenges relating to the distinction between gig and unorganized workers, and its rulings in the coming years will further shape this area of law.

In the previous chapters we have discussed a number of labour laws that are applicable in India, including the new codes that are meant to reform and simplify other existing labour laws.

Knowledge of existing labour laws is important for all employees since they may be relevant to their current workplace conditions and relations with the employers. It is hoped that reading this book has provided some help in this regard.

About the authors

Siva Prasad Bose is a retired electrical engineer and writer of introductory guides on aspects of law in India. He is retired after many years of service in Uttar Pradesh Power Corporation Limited (UPPCL, formerly UPSEB). He received his engineering degree from Jadavpur University, Kolkata and has a law degree from Meerut University, Meerut and a BSc from MMH College Ghaziabad. His interests lie in the fields of family law, civil law, law of contracts, and any areas of law related to electric power related issues.

Joy Bose holds an LLM from Golden Gate University, San Francisco, and is a data scientist by profession with a strong interest in making complex legal and financial topics accessible to general readers.

Other books by Siva Prasad Bose

Introduction to Wills and Probate

Senior Citizens Abuse in India: And what to do about it

Introduction to Negotiable Instruments: As per Indian laws

Introduction to Marriage Laws in India

Managing Court Cases with Mental Strength

Self-Publish Books and E-Books in India

Delays in Court Cases in India

Introduction to Patents and Patent Law in India

Introduction to Property Law in India

Introduction to Tort Law in India

Did you love *Introduction to Labour Laws in India*? Then you should read *Introduction to Tort Law in India*[1] by Siva Prasad Bose!

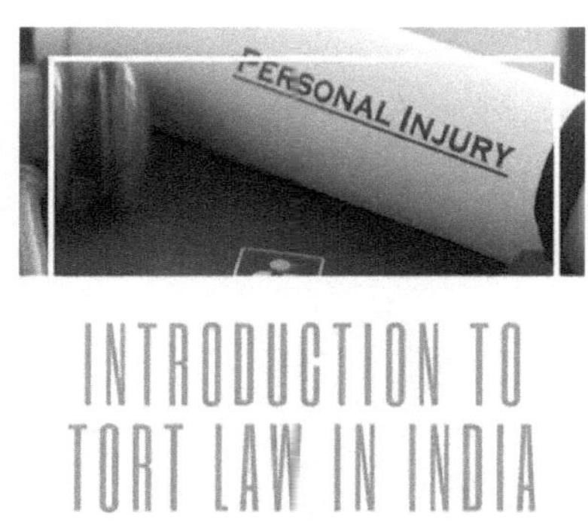

[2]

Tort law shapes everyday life in India, from slip-and-fall accidents and noisy neighbors to online defamation and state negligence. Yet for most people, it remains an unfamiliar corner of the legal system. *Introduction to Tort Law in India* changes that.

Written in plain language and grounded in the Indian legal context, this book walks you through the full landscape of civil wrongs, what they are, how courts handle them, and what

---

1. https://books2read.com/u/4jPdzo

2. https://books2read.com/u/4jPdzo

remedies are available to you. Whether you're a law student, a legal professional, or simply someone who wants to understand your rights, this book is built for you.

What's Inside

Drawing on real case laws and practical examples, the book covers the core torts — negligence, nuisance, defamation, trespass, and malicious prosecution — alongside important topics like vicarious liability, constitutional torts, and consumer protection. A dedicated chapter on emerging digital-age torts addresses online defamation, AI liability, environmental harm, and the growing intersection of technology and civil rights.

The book also includes procedural essentials: how the Code of Civil Procedure applies to tort claims, how to send a legal notice, and how to navigate both civil and criminal dimensions of a tort.

Who This Book Is For

Law students seeking a clear, exam-friendly overview of Indian tort law

Legal practitioners looking for a concise reference on case law and doctrine

General readers who want to understand their rights and available remedies

Anyone dealing with property disputes, negligence claims, or civil grievances

Introduction to Tort Law in India is a practical gateway to a vital — and increasingly relevant — area of Indian civil law.

Read more at https://sivaprasadbose.wordpress.com/.

About the Author

Siva Prasad Bose is an electrical engineer by profession. He is currently retired after many years of service in Uttar Pradesh Power Corporation Limited. He received his engineering degree from Jadavpur University, Kolkata and has a law degree from Meerut University, Meerut. His interests lie in the fields of family law, civil law, law of contracts, and any areas of law related to power electricity related issues.

Read more at https://sivaprasadbose.wordpress.com/.